HUMAN
SPIRIT
ORACLE

HUMAN
SPIRIT
ORACLE

LEARNING TO RECONNECT

Jena Dellagrottaglia

ROCKPOOL

A Rockpool book
PO Box 252
Summer Hill
NSW 2130
Australia

rockpoolpublishing.com

Follow us! **f** ☉ rockpoolpublishing
Tag your images with #rockpoolpublishing

ISBN: 9781922785176

Published in 2023 by Rockpool Publishing
Copyright text © Jena Dellagrottaglia & Laurence Toner 2023
Copyright images © Jena Dellagrottaglia 2023
Copyright design © Rockpool Publishing 2023

Design by Sara Lindberg, Rockpool Publishing
Edited by Kaitlyn Smith

Printed and bound in China
10 9 8 7 6 5 4 3 2 1

CONTENTS

INTRODUCTION

Welcome to the *Human Spirit Oracle*! This deck is about what we universally go through as humans. Sometimes we are too deep in our circumstances to see, or realise, that although our journey is unique the circumstances along the way connect us. This 44-card deck gives insight into what it means to be human and offers guidance on where a person is in their journey.

The purpose of this deck is to remind us that we are all connected, but first and foremost, we are human. It's time to find the spark and rekindle our humanity. It's important that we get back to us, to our souls, to our kind minds.

This deck is a vivacious culmination of art, soul, and insight from one human to another, not only on a spiritual level, but on a human level. The design of this deck is focused on diversity, in both ethnicity and gender, and the guidance is a universal connection of our humanity.

Humans are infinitely complex, but how we connect is basic to the core. The *Human Spirit Oracle* is a means to get back to the basics; to get back to spirit. This deck is not to predict or to tell your future, this deck is on the *Human Spirit Oracle*, something EVERYONE suffers from. We are all unique and whether we feel 100 per cent justified in our beliefs, thoughts or just everyday way of thinking about other people it is hard to know what we can or cannot do, say or be. In a click, a scroll or a swipe we can be connected to a myriad of things, people and places. But ask yourself, is this authentic? We all believe our voices are the loudest, we all have a moment or more of suffering from FOMO, wanting to be an all-inclusive, yet separate entity. When you get right down to it, we are ALL HUMAN, and everyone should be treated as such. Until that happens things will remain the same.

So, open your heart, your mind, walk a mile in someone else's shoes and let's begin an exploration into the *Human Spirit Oracle*.

A PERSONAL NOTE

We wanted to take a moment to thank you for purchasing our deck and believing in our vision. We are so filled with gratitude.

PLEASE TAG US IN INSTAGRAM POSTS

jena_dellagrottaglia | wordsmithedits

We will be sure to feature in our story when we see them.

HOW TO USE
THE CARDS

Welcome human, guess what? If you are reading this, you have stumbled upon a not so secret secret... You suffer from being human, just like the rest of us. The purpose of this deck is to bring to light that we all are first and foremost a human, and, though our journeys are unique, the trials we face connect us. Find the spark and rekindle your humanity, get back to 'us', to our souls, to our minds, authentically. There is enough minutiae and poppycock out there, making it easy for us to forget we are all in this together.

We have created this deck from not only a place of love, but also with the best intentions for every human from all walks of life to feel comfortable using it.

To work with these cards, you just have to have a clear intention, an open mind, and a desire to connect with yourself. We suggest meditation, exercise and dance. Whatever it takes to relax you and free your mind.

REVERSE MEANING:

The *Human Spirit Oracle* was created with two meanings for each card, and that is why we have provided an upright as well as reversed message. Both messages are meant to help you along your human experience, and there are no rules or restrictions on how to use this deck. Use your intuition or set an intention with the deck on how you would like to use it, and work with the message that speaks best to you.

DAILY MESSAGE CARD PULL

1. Focus on your shuffle, how the cards feel in your hands. Don't rush the process, really connect with the cards.
2. Ask the oracle, universe or your higher power a question. Remember this is more of a human deck as opposed to a spiritual deck.
3. Select your card after making one single stack and fanning them out. Decide where you feel compelled to pick from.
4. If you feel the message doesn't 'make sense or apply' don't worry it will at some point in your day.

You might not always understand it immediately, and that is ok. Trust the cards, and your intuition. Go about your day and remember the card and its message. Somewhere along the way it will make perfect sense to you.

BEGINNING, MIDDLE AND END CARD PULL

1. Connect to yourself, really feel in tune with you. Trust in your intuition.
2. Shuffle your oracle cards and ask yourself for knowledge in the reading. Stay focused on your question or search for insight.
3. Select your three cards, however you feel most comfortable choosing.

These cards may be lessons, or reminders, ways for spirit to let us know that we are not alone, and that we are all cosmically connected. Keep these cards in mind as you go about your week, paying attention to the sequence and how the first card relates to the beginning of your week, how the second card correlates to your mid-week, and how the final third card corresponds to the end of your week.

WEEK IN DEPTH PULL

1. Connect to yourself, perhaps meditate while you handle the cards. Have knowledge that your intuition is on point.
2. Shuffle your oracle cards and ask for clarity, knowledge and guidance for this week. Remember this is all about the human experience, but part of being human is that deep soulful knowledge.
3. Select your seven cards for each day of the week, however you feel comfortable doing so. Some choose to make three stacks and pull from there, and some fan the cards out picking those they are most drawn to.

Like in the Beginning, Middle and End Card Pull, these cards may be lessons, or reminders, or a tone for the day. Keep these cards in mind as you go about your day and week. These cards aren't prophecies, they are a tool in your human toolbox to insight joy, give you guidance and build your connection with your own human experience.

We recommend these spreads, but at the end of the day, it is whatever works best for you.

We also encourage you to try a spread you create. Please share your spreads with us on social media. Remember there is only one rule here and that's Don't Be a D!CK.

THE
CARDS

ANY WAY
(THE WIND BLOWS)

I am so easy… ummm… mind out of the gutter please. I am going with the flow, letting myself just go where things take me and swaying along the journey with the utmost trust. Do you easily bend like the branches of a great willow tree to what surrounds you? Does the breeze softly sway you and take you any way the wind blows? If not, then perhaps it is time to lean into it, let's get limber and go with the flow of the universe! You will find that life can be a peaceful and abundant journey if you trust in yourself and the universe's plan. There is no use in getting caught up in things that are simply out of your control. Take a moment today to sway away, move and learn along your path. You will find that, without resistance, life can be much less stressful, or even feel like it is flowing easily.

So, try it out, plant your feet to the earth, arms in the air and just give in to the sway. Remember if you do not bend you will break!

REVERSE

Oh well look at you, just like a feather blowing all over the place. We love your trust in the universe, but you also need to recognise when it is time to stand your ground and change the things you do not like that are coming your way. Sometimes all the universe wants of us is to stick up for ourselves, to find our worth and demand it. If you are always just playing along, if you are always just going along the path of least resistance because you are afraid of what might happen then like the feather you will always just be blown anyway the winds take you.

It is time now to stand in your power and the trick to that is balance. The balance of knowing when it is time to rely on your roots, or when it is time to go with the flow. Even a river knows when to bend, or find a better path, so if this plane isn't going where you'd like, take the next one!

AM I BLUE?

Hey, you turn that frown upside down.

With all the fear tactics that are going on in the world today it is easy to get caught up in sorrow and worry. It is understandable that every now and again we give into our emotions; we cry, feel sad, get scared and even isolate ourselves from our friends and loved ones. We are asking you to not wallow or get stuck in these feelings. Mental health is a part of self-care and nurturing yourself is exactly what you need at this moment. Recognise when you have spent too long in the deep blue, and if you feel like you are drowning in sorrow, please seek a life preserver.

There is no shame in your game, and it is ok to not be ok! There is such a stigma attached to mental health and wellness, do not let pride get in the way of self-care. An act of self-kindness is sometimes all we need to chase our blues away.

REVERSE

Blue ain't your colour! Have you become so numb to everything around you that you feel absolutely nothing for the state of the world?

Sometimes, we get so caught up in our feelings, we disassociate with them and ignore them because we would rather not feel them; especially when they make us feel blue. But… they are called feelings for a reason, they are meant to be experienced, they often highlight lessons that need to be learned. If we are constantly ignoring our feelings, then we are not completing assignments that the universe has assigned us. When we 'live' our lives suppressing our emotions and feelings we walk through life like a zombie.

It is often easier to ignore our feelings than feel them, especially when they make us feel blue. Don't be the class clown flunking out of your own life. Be the over achiever, that A+ student in the front row.

COMMUNE WITH NATURE

Does a bear poop in the woods? Let's go on a hike and find out! Get off the phone and computer screens and take some time to connect with the natural world… AKA nature! When we are constantly connected to our devices, we lose that primal connection to the natural order. Mother Nature has given us everything that we need, but as a society we have turned to materialistic things and technology. When we get anxious or feel trapped, the first thing we say is 'I need some air'.

When our worlds become too much, we can find peace and solace in nature.

Take time today to breathe in some fresh air, take in nature and sit with your old friend Mother Nature. Take your shoes off, let the soles of your feet touch the earth. Your worries will sink into the soil and, at least for the moment, you can breathe a little easier.

REVERSE

Organic, no preservatives, no GMOs, gluten free… you've done the work, you're composting like a champ! So, why won't your friends jump on board? Sometimes we can be extreme without even realising, especially when we are sharing something that we are passionate about and believe in. Maybe your friends are overwhelmed by all the information, and they are just scared to make that first step. Maybe they just haven't had the opportunity to connect with nature like you have.

Whether it is composting or the fight against global warming, take this card as a sign that sometimes the best way to reach someone isn't a 'verbal essay', sometimes it can be as simple as gifting a cute recyclable composting bucket or bike ride share membership to a friend. You live your life outside of 'the box', if you can apply that to all your passions, the world will be a better place.

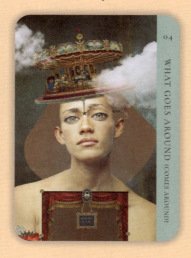

WHAT GOES AROUND
(COMES AROUND)

Round and round we go, where we stop… nobody knows!!! When we go through a lot, it takes a lot to continue to do good and to be good. Whether you believe in karma or not, its practice is based on being a good person through spreading positivity and good deeds, both to ourselves and others. Today spread some kindness, smile at a stranger, compliment a friend, or even just hold the door for someone behind you. Always remember that what goes around comes around. I promise that when you do good, you feel good.

Ever have someone compliment your shoes, your smile, or even your attitude? Didn't it just brighten up your day? You carry an extra bit of confidence in your step, a wider smile. This is a wonderful thing to send out like a boomerang into the world. It always seems to return exactly when you need it most.

REVERSE

Ever heard of karma? What kind of energy have you been tossing out into the universe lately? Is it the best possible version of yourself that you want to show, or are you walking around putting out poppycock? I am sure you are saying to yourself 'Come on… we all have off days', but even in those moments we can make a conscious choice to send out a boomerang of what we hope to get back karmically. Remember we are all in this together! We have heard that a lot recently but the plain truth of it is… we are all we have, all of us together.

So, you woke up on the wrong side of the bed? Do you wake up and go to your local coffee shop and sneer and mutter because they are out of oat milk? Do you take it out on the barista (for example)? Remember you just put that negative energy out into the universe, and now may have made another person have a lousy morning. If you wake up on the wrong side of the bed, think of all the blessings you have or could receive today instead of spreading around your hogwash. Remember what you put out into the universe may not come back today will eventually make its way back to you. Do not get stuck on a merry-go-round of malarkey, send out some kindness, some love and peace.

FISHBOWL

Are you swimming in a fishbowl, watching everyone outside of it truly living life? What are you afraid of? That you won't be able to function out there, or perhaps it looks too scary, or dangerous, or even strange? Remember we are here to have a human experience. To touch other people in big and small ways. If we are always isolated or 'safe' in our own spaces, then we lose out on the beauty of the universe. Reiterate to yourself today that you will have an honest and authentic human experience, and no two humans or experiences are exactly alike. This is the beauty of mingling and leaping out of the water.

Imagine the adventures you could have if you just get out of the fishbowl and really connect on a genuine human level. If you are always experiencing life from your fishbowl, then you will never know some of the most amazing things that can happen. By staying put you limit your own human experience! The fishbowl will always be there to welcome you back, but the sea is big, and vast. It is time to put on those flippers and take a swim in new waters!

REVERSE

Is that caffeine or just your charismatic personality coming through? Clearly you are the big fish in a little pond but remember to not be imposing to others around you. Are you feeling especially social today? That is great, but please keep in mind that some people are used to swimming alone and not in a school. Learn to read others' social cues. Does the person you are interacting with seem to be one of these solitary swimmers? If so then let us remember boundaries and allow that person to open up in their own time. If you are sucking up all the air in the room then others will have to find some elsewhere.

If you want someone to open up, then try making a safe space for them to do that. Sometimes you can do that by just leaving space, a breath, or silence for them. We have all felt like a fish out of water at some point, and you have since been through it and found your stroke. It is time to make room for others to do the same. When they see the 'big fish' making room for them they will feel acknowledged and safe!

UNLOCK YOUR MIND

Did you hear that? That is the sound of your mind unlocking. We have been hearing this term lately 'a Karen or a Ken'. What exactly does this 'Karen and Ken' mean? These are people who feel like their way is the only way, and refuse to budge on expanding their thoughts, point of view, or sometimes plainly seeing the facts. Take some time today to unlock and set free all of your possibilities. It is believed that we use about 10 per cent of our brain. Think about that, 10 per cent!

Are you trying to stick with the same thought patterns without ever really expanding, or even exploring new possibilities? If you could learn one new thing today, or perhaps see someone else's point of view, someone that you think you have absolutely nothing in common with, you might just touch on a real human moment of seeing things you never thought possible. Think of it like putting on a pair of glasses that you never realised you even needed.

REVERSE

Your door is shut, deadbolted, chained, knob locked and your curtains closed tight. Is there nothing that anyone can say that can make you look at things from a different perspective? What has brought you to this point? Have you learned all there is to learn and are done growing and evolving?

We are human, and with this comes life lessons, new thoughts, evolution of your humanity and CHANGE. If you never take a moment to hear or see something from someone else's point of view, then you are limiting yourself from growing and from connecting to others. Hurt people hurt people, and if you are hiding behind that locked door… so is your hurt. It is time to let go, it is time to step back, and it is time to unlock that door, open your mind to new things and new perspectives. Take a moment to put yourself in someone else's shoes, even if they are super sensible and not your style.

ALL ABOARD

Next stop...With so many causes, protests and ideologies nowadays, it is so easy to hop aboard the newest 'trends' and 'fund me campaigns'. It is important to understand that not every cause is what's best for us all. Knowledge is power and if you are feeling like hopping aboard a cause, have your facts, which in this day and age might be harder to find then one would think. It is great to be passionate for the world and to have a passion for change but be sure it is the type of change that benefits humanity. By humanity I mean the world, and the earth as a whole; not just you, your family or neighbourhood.

We aren't saying don't mow your neighbour's lawn, or don't volunteer at the co-op, but when a cause limits the rights of others or dictates the choices of people then let's get knowledgeable about all the facts! Let's do our research from reputable sources, because uncle Jesse is a great person... but how many books has he read in the last year? With social media blaring at you with what you should believe and support, it is hard to sometimes find the right track to the best train out of the station.

REVERSE

Can we see your ticket? Are you feeling overwhelmed with all the causes, hashtags and being told what to care about? So much so that you are just done and want to believe that someone else will fight for the cause? It is worth having a cause you are passionate about and knowing it takes more than a village to make a change. Find that cause, be sure it is right and support it, be educated about it, spread that knowledge and be an advocate. You can be the person spreading the message to friends and family, sharing your perspective and message is a great way to be a part of the bigger picture. It takes a village, and in a village every voice matters, so does yours! Don't get discouraged, or overwhelmed, because even the smallest light dispels darkness.

Not all causes are one size fits all. Some causes may inspire you to give more than just a donation, while others are as simple as a monthly payment and maybe a shoutout on your social media.

Decide for yourself how involved you want to be with your cause. This will help to eliminate those overwhelmed nerves.

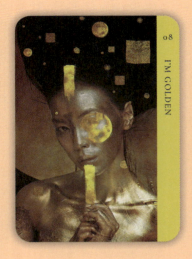

08

I'M GOLDEN

Solid 18 karat, 24K, or just gold plated? What does this mean to you?
Are you golden in a way where you have dipped everything in your
life into a shiny over coating, leaving you to feel lacklustre inside?
Or are you truly golden, from the inside out? Meaning you have
tended to your needs both mentally and physically. You have put in
the work, the self-love and have checked your mind, body and soul,
and are feeling above all else full of that golden shine! Know your
worth. If you are unsure about something you feel, do a little digging
until you get to the heart of the matter. A little personal mining if

you will. Sometimes we need to hack away at the stone to get to our glimmer and shine.

When we shine, we leave a little glow wherever we go. Remember even gold must be pulled from a dull rock.

REVERSE

What is priceless and golden to you? When you truly get down to it and think about it, is it only the material things and physical comforts that come to mind? What do these 'things' mean to you, why do you associate so much value to them? Is it because you are using them to fill a void? Or are you perhaps worried about keeping up with other people around you, with an image you have created in your head? There are also the pressures of social media, and how we present ourselves, but behind all the filters and facades are humans who are hurting and putting on a show for others.

Are you trying to keep up with others on social media and what they seem to have? If so, ask yourself why, and what is truly of value to you? Instead of subscribing to them, you need to subscribe to yourself. Take some time to look inward to mine what is a truly precious commodity; yourself.

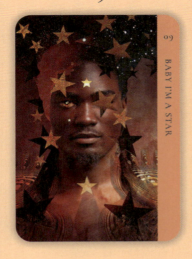

09

BABY I'M A STAR

Hold on, where are my sunglasses at? You are a star baby, shine on, shine on! Sometimes when we are so full of inner light, we cannot see it for ourselves. You have a certain *je ne sais quoi* that everyone can see and feel, it is magnetic! A certain magic that attracts the right people and circumstances to you. The stars just seem to align for you, the dots connect, and when you put your mind to something it just falls into place. When you have star power it is important to share it.

Sharing your light, your shine and gifts with others allows us all to grow and evolve along with you. When one of us shines, we all shine, but you are the lead role. So, step into the spotlight and take a bow, because today you are ALL that boo. CUT, that's a wrap! Get this baby a Hollywood star on the Walk of Fame!

REVERSE

Me, Me, Me, Me, Me! Is this what we have come to as a society now? Do you have enough followers? Likes? Do you look flawless? Is your life HUGE enough to be a star on social media? Is this really what has become important to you? We have become reduced to selfie filters, living above our means, and not showing our authentic self to the world. Are you stuck living in a virtual world spending your entire existence on your phone, tablet, or laptop? Stop and realise this does not validate you, nor does it build character.

It is ok to cruise, but don't make it a road trip and destination. All of these filters and airbrushes have made us, as a human race, become more dog-eat-dog and numb to what is really around us. Take a look around you today outside of social media and find out what is truly in your life that you can be thankful for; what honestly makes you a star.

ROAD LESS TRAVELLED

Beep, beep! Are you stuck in traffic trying to go the same way as everyone else? Travelling at the same speed, which is stop and go? Try taking the road less travelled, you will be surprised how this road will lead you to undiscovered parts of yourself, and help you find the most authentic you rather than being in the same lane or fast lane trying to follow the 'social norm' or the short cut. It is important to know the side streets and back roads of you, because sometimes the scenery is new and alluring. The new path helping you find wonderful new avenues of you and who you truly are. Trust me, when you feel like you do not recognise or like yourself, it is usually because you are not being who you truly are, and somewhere inside your authentic self is just trying to set off a rescue flare.

Pay attention to the signal and make a turn off to your road less travelled. Trust us, we are here for individual experiences, human road trips perhaps. Pack a lunch and take your time during the journey.

REVERSE

Driver's licence and registration please!!! You are on the right path, truly being your most authentic you. We ABSOLUTELY love this about you! You have been enjoying the journey, finding all those little hidden treasures on your road to Humanville. Don't worry about being in the fast lane, set your cruise control and make your own way. You have charted your own course, written your own map, and sometimes this can be a lonely solitary journey, and that is ok. Put some tunes on that you are too embarrassed to play when others are in the car and sing your heart out!

When you have reached your destination, it is ok to send your coordinates to others. It's not your directions they need, but a beacon to start a journey of their own on the road less travelled. Until then, remember, there is no road map or GPS needed right now, stay on your course, because the destination is an authentic life lived!

MIDAS TOUCH

You have that GOLDEN touch! You have worked hard, or perhaps just inherited this amazing skill to touch all that you desire, and it turns golden, and shiny. Yours: no strings attached? Does it feel rewarding? Or do you come to just expect little morsels of gold to form at your beck and call. Let's take a moment to think about instant gratification without gratitude. It is important to know your blessings and take a moment to give thanks for them. If you have more than enough, maybe consider donating monthly to your favourite cause.

Sprinkle that gold all over like glitter and let others have a blessing to give thanks for. Remember that old expression 'share the wealth', this is a great time to practice that age-old saying. It will bring you great joy... I promise.

REVERSE

Everything you put your finger, mind, or intentions on turns to something grey, perhaps without value? Maybe you are looking too closely at the dirt and grit. Take a moment to realise that the most beautiful of gems come from the earth, caked in grit, dirt, perhaps even you must capture a few worms before you realise you need to polish off the debris to see what value truly lies there.

Remember to set intentions, be brave, and always remember what you put out in thought is what you get. Raise your personal 'price tag' out of clearance to one of a kind. Because, baby, you are absolutely worth it. Remember patience when you are mining for gold.

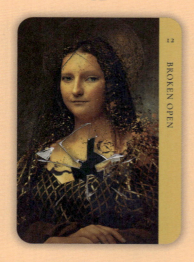

BROKEN OPEN

You must have some cracks to let the light shine through!!!

Have you been through something that tore you into pieces, that broke you down to nothing? When we break it makes space for growth. Like a dense forest there can be no sun for new growth, but when one tree falls, or breaks, it allows the warming sun to penetrate the canopy and feed the roots.

You've been through enough; it is time to feed your roots and step into the sun. Remember that sometimes you must tear something down to rebuild a better 'home'. The same is true for us. If we have been through life shattering events do not get stuck in the ruins of what was, instead build a fabulous new dwelling.

Never underestimate the kerb appeal of a renovated home!

REVERSE

Do you feel broken, like your life is a thousand pieces drifting on a breeze? It is time, like an old piñata you must break open to reveal all those yummy morsels that are inside of you. Just as a mosaic, our true beauty is discovered when we can look at the whole picture. We are greater than the sum of our parts, the tiny broken pieces that make us, created us.

You are in the thick of it, the doubt, the fear, focused on the tiny broken pieces that make up the whole. Take a breath and remember that YOU got this far, and YOU are stronger than you believe.

13

HIT YOUR TARGET

READY, AIM, FIRE! We see you have been practicing your skill of hitting your mark. Well done, because whatever project or adventure you are on know that you are so close to that bullseye. You are hitting that target. It might feel strange when everything falls into place, everything clicks, but you worked hard for this.

It is ok to enjoy success, enjoy the journey, and take a moment to pat yourself on the back! Skills take time, practice and patience. Hitting your target is no different. You know what you want and exactly how to get it. There is absolutely no shame in your game.

REVERSE

Hitting your mark takes concentration. Are you distracted lately? Are you being torn in 12 different directions?

You cannot give one hundred per cent to 12 different things at the same time and expect a good result. It is time to prioritise and learn to say no! You have your own goals that need to be met rather than always assisting in side quests for other humans and their goals. Sometimes you need to be selfish in order to be a better version of you. Just like safety rules on a plane you must get your own oxygen before helping someone else.

Now go hit your target.

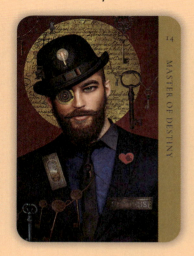

14

MASTER OF DESTINY

AHOY THERE! You are at the helm of your ship, choosing the course and making the choices.

You can chart your own map and decide where you want to venture. It won't always be smooth sailing, sometimes the waters can get choppy and rough. That is ok. Because, lucky for you, you captain this ship. Trust in yourself, believe you can achieve your goals and dreams.

It's ok to get scared or feel unsure. Remember, when you are on the right course your sea legs won't fail you.

Funny that we are travelling these many destinations to create our best destiny. Perhaps that is where the word destinations comes from? And now give yourself a high five for charting these uncharted waters, and fully understanding that you are the Master of your Destiny!

REVERSE

Oh, hi there, are you just walking in a circle waiting for some other person to tell you where your destiny is?

What is your plan? What is the goal?

You cannot get from point A to point B if you don't even know where you are starting from. If you walk the same circle without changing course, you will create a trench size hole that you might find it hard to get out of. Let's take time to assess where you are, and where you want to go. If you are nervous to chart your trail in ink, then let's try chalk, easily erased when you feel a wind of change in your sails.

Take hold of the wheel and become the Master of your own Destiny.

Shed the labels placed on you by others or by your past and create your own path.

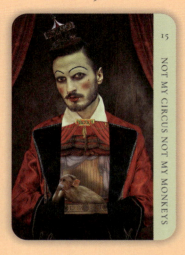

15

NOT MY CIRCUS
NOT MY MONKEYS

Sheesh you there with the monkey. GET OFF MY LAWN!

Why are you always hanging on to someone else's problem? Is it boundaries, do you suffer from co-dependency, or are you a hero at the expense of your own happiness?

We spend a lot of time speaking about and on other people's problems, because they are easier to see and solve than our own. Some people also thrive on drama, so self-inflicted, and they want to make you part of their three-ring circus. Tossing you from their trapeze of chaos into their habitat of monkeys.

Next time you start to swing from someone else's problem, take a moment and say 'Not my Circus, Not my Monkeys' and take a step back.

REVERSE

Are you always in chaos and asking for friends and family to come and save you from your problems?

First things first, are these issues something you create, perhaps because you thrive off drama, or you need to know someone will come to your rescue? If that is indeed the case, it's time to re-evaluate your own self-worth, as well as your own problem-solving skills.

Seriously why does chaos and drama seem to be at your heels? It's ok to vent on friends once in a while, or even ask for help on occasion. However, now is the time to take responsibility for the problems you create. It isn't always fair to ask the people around you to come to your rescue. It isn't their circus and those aren't their monkeys.

16

HOT HEAD

Talk about explosive, hunny you are just a little powder keg ready to go off at a moment's notice. KABOOM! What is it that has you so heated? We know there are so many facets of life (especially now) that just make that temper mercury rise and sometimes our emotions get the best of us. Maybe you are holding onto a grudge, or an argument. If so, just let that sh!t go, nothing good has ever come out of holding onto a grudge, it makes you cranky, difficult and it's downright unhealthy. Maybe you are just angry with the state of the world. Well guess what? You can only change your immediate world, that which deals with your everyday life. So, let's start with letting our fists unclench.

If you approach life with positivity, kindness and patience your environment almost instantly changes. It becomes calmer, more compassionate and frankly just easier. (Try some meditation, some art, writing or boxing. Just find an outlet for the anger that is healthy.) If you find you cannot quell this heat, we ask that you seek a lifesaver.

A group for anger management, therapy, something that can help you move forward and out of this fire.

REVERSE

We've got live explosives here, CAUTION! Passive aggressive has always reminded me of a car insurance name. Let's discuss your needs to avoid confrontation, by pouting, appeasing, or just plain avoiding a situation someone asks of you. Here is a good time to assert yourself (no explosion please). It's ok to say no and set boundaries. When you do, you may be surprised that the whole world continues to move on, and so can you. There may be people in your life who back away because you set boundaries, but that is because most of those people, the ones who cannot respect your wishes and boundaries, are not your true friends.

If people want to know why, you do not need to explain your reasons. If something being asked of you makes you uncomfortable, or maybe you just don't feel like doing something, try calmly declining. Trust me you will feel so relieved!

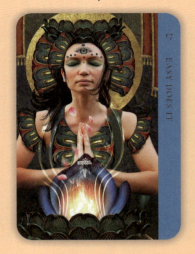

17

EASY DOES IT

INHALE the good sh!t, EXHALE the bad sh!t. We love this sassy mantra because they are absolutely words to live your life by. Take a breath and slow down. In the breath there is a stillness, a moment of peace. It is important, as a human, to recharge not just our minds, but our body and soul as well. You cannot always be giving one hundred per cent. Not only is it exhausting to you, but it also can be exhausting to those around you.

When you are feeling overwhelmed, just remember to hit the pause button. There are so many fun ways to do this! You can take a bubble bath and just sit in the stillness around you, powering down and recharging. Maybe you prefer meditating, gardening, or curling up for a cat nap. Take at least ten minutes a day to unwind and let go of the demands and stress of life.

REVERSE

Well, hello there, are you on the couch? Have you been sitting there all day? Well good for you, you have recognised the need to take a day on slow mode. Be careful though to not get stuck there. Sometimes we can fall into a pit of lazy procrastination and just linger there, or sometimes it is just those super comfy couches that swallow you whole when you sit there. The point is to know the difference.

We recommend a nice invigorating shower for starters, then perhaps a jaunt to your favourite cafe or restaurant, followed by an evening stroll around your block. Sometimes we all need a reset, or restart to get back in sync.

18

I'M POSSIBLE

Yas Queen (or King)! You are a strong and beautiful person. Sometimes we can forget that in the static that is our everyday experiences. It also feels great when we are reminded of that from outside sources, a type of validation. Every now and again we just need to take a moment to reflect, give ourselves some self-love, and remember how amazing we are!

Look in that mirror and see your full potential.

Try simple affirmations to yourself:

'I am possible.'

'I am enough.'

'I am a radiant being of love and light.'

Whatever your affirmation might be, repeat it nine times, reiterating how AMAZING you are!

REVERSE

It's easier to commiserate than celebrate.

What are you telling yourself today? Are you filled with self-doubt, feeling less than? We have all been here but let's focus on something positive.

Maybe something happened to you in life, or someone said something negative and hurtful. We are asking you to look at yourself in the mirror, find one thing today that you love about yourself (physical or otherwise), and just make a lovely, kind mantra or affirmation about this aspect, then repeat it nine times. We hope that soon you know you are very possible, and your self-confidence will be through the roof.

19

BUTTERFLY EFFECT

What you do today can linger into your tomorrows, and perhaps someone else's tomorrows as well. It is like when someone says something negative to you and you carry it through your day and then pass that ick onto someone else. This is why it is important to think before you act, remember every action has an equal and opposite reaction.

Let's do a quick analogy: someone far away wakes up in the morning and steps on a tack. That puts them in a bloody foul mood, so maybe they get rude with their spouse or partner, setting the tone for the rest of their day. Their partner then goes out into the world to work. They now ruffle those wings spreading that same poo poo attitude onto a fellow co-worker. That co-worker did nothing wrong and has been making a product that is important to something of safety that will be sold all over the world. But, instead of quality control, they are blindly doing the job while venting to a co-worker… this gizmo then gets packed and shipped with all the other gizmos somewhere halfway across the world. Someone buys it and uses it for… well you see where this goes and continues to go. Long story short (too late hahaha), are you spreading poop?

Awww that's unfortunate because those poop filled wings just splattered into someone else's day. Stop and consider the consequences of your actions.

REVERSE

Oh hunny, make a difference, leave your mark. Toss something wonderful into the day and see where it goes. Just like glitter (did we cancel glitter yet!) fill your hands with twinkle, shine and joy then let it go into the wind and fly into the air. Let it touch as many people as possible. Isn't that so much better than slinging caca?

When you are able to put out beauty and share light it creates a butterfly effect of amazing karma, of smiles and of pure magic.

20

SUPPORT SYSTEM

You are awesome and we hope you are finding that the people you surround yourself with lift you up when you are soaring, as well as comfort you when you are down. Everyone needs a support system, a true-blue friend, a therapist, a group, or a lover. Surround yourself with this sort of person. It is a wonderful thing to watch those we love thrive and flourish. Strong arms to hold you, a helping hand to lift you up! As if it was part of your own being, not even a thought given.

Community is so important, even if it is a community of two or three. Take pride in yourself, this means it is ok to be choosy with the people you surround yourself with. You are a one-of-a-kind gift, hunny. You deserve a wonderful support system filled with love, pride and truth. If someone is not there for the good and bad times, then what exactly are they there for?

REVERSE

Some people should come with a huge skull and crossbones label, like poison or toxins!

Who are you surrounding yourself with? It is easier to commiserate than celebrate. Do you ever notice how people will spread poop when you are low? It usually means they are trying to make themselves feel better for their shortcomings, issues, or just their lingering poop.

Some people will deviate you to lesser things as opposed to greater accomplishments. Be wary. Do the people in your circle lift you up? Are they wreaking havoc on your emotional and physical state? Sometimes when we are in the thick of a toxic situation it is very hard to see it for what it is. This is a good time to have your sh!t detecting glasses on and get the heck out of there. Find yourself in new surroundings. True blues will want to watch you thrive and grow and be happy for all your successes.

21

SIREN'S SONG

Ahhh the lure of the Siren's Song… it beckons you in and calls you with the promise of beauty, treasure and magic. But not everything is as it seems. Before you follow the call make sure you know where it is you are going, or what it is that you are agreeing to. Most of the time if something seems too good to be true, it is.

Ask questions, educate yourself, seek that knowledge before you jump headfirst into something. If you have a gut reaction, or a little voice in your head, or just a moment of second guessing something, then lean into that. Ask yourself 'Why am I feeling this?' Is it because of a past trauma or is it your intuition telling you that this might not be all that it is cracked up to be?

Whether it is a purchase, a situation, or a human interaction, just take a moment to really think about what you are doing before you do it. Know exactly what it is you are getting into, because it could save you a lot of time and energy in the long haul.

REVERSE

This song falls upon deaf ears.

You have been misled before and are not so easily swayed by the enchanting melody or the shiny baubles. Some might even say you are jaded or cynical and passing up some amazing opportunities in being so. Maybe today, instead of putting on noise cancelling headphones, we can give what tries to call us in a closer look?

Sometimes there is something amazing being offered to us (whether it be an object, an experience, or a person), suss it out and maybe give it a chance. Let your intuition be your guide on this one. Not everything that tempts us bites! Sometimes being too cautious makes us miss out on some of the universe's most beautiful gifts or experiences.

22

WALLFLOWER

Oh, there you are…I almost didn't notice you blending into that wall there! You have made it to the party, now get up off that wall, mingle, dance and find joy.

I know sometimes it might be hard meeting new people, coming out of your introverted shell, while trying not to be seen. But you never know you might meet someone interesting, have a good laugh, dance until you sweat.

At least you can say you got off the wall and gave it a try.

REVERSE

Are you so afraid to be seen, you do not take any chances?

Are you feeling unworthy? Scared? Shy?

EVERYONE goes through this at one time or another, perhaps you need to take baby steps away from your comfort zone of the wall, and that is ok. Everyone at their own speed. But remember to at least try life to the fullest.

23

EYE TO EYE

I spy with my little eye… you!

Do you view things from other perspectives?

Trying to see eye to eye with the beings in your world?

Remember reality is all relative to the human experience. In your reality there is only your truth, and all you can do is try to understand someone else's truth. Seeing eye to eye, or at least respecting someone's reality, can make life less of an argument or competition and more of a meaningful existence. It is easy to forget that we all see things differently. Remember all eyes are different and see things from their individual point of view. It might do you some good to take the time to listen to someone else's version, and help to expand your own horizons, or at least realise where they are coming from.

Just think of the game I spy, someone sees something from a window, that same window you are looking through, but you don't always have the same focal point at first.

REVERSE

Are you in a constant battle, locking horns with others who are trying to give you their view on things?

Are you refusing to even see things from another perspective?

We like to call this condition 'Optirectal-itis' (you can figure this one out). You will not have very many deep or meaningful moments if you refuse to see eye to eye, or at least respect someone else's point of view. Sometimes we do not need to see things the same, but it could enrich a relationship or situation to let someone know you can see where they are coming from and understand it.

So, take those blinders off and look out of a different window today.

24

HEAD IN THE CLOUDS

Well, hello up there! How is the view from up there?

Are you living in a dreamy, almost obscure day to day? Having dreams is what makes the world go round. But do not get so lost in the dream that you forget your reality. It is easy to get lost in the fantasy of it all.

While dreaming is amazing, you must take different avenues to get to them (setting and manifesting your intentions). Perhaps a vision board will help you get a little more grounded to manifest your dreams, as opposed to having your head in the clouds and just waiting for your dreams to manifest without taking any real part in making them come true.

REVERSE

You are so grounded, and living the daily grind, you have forgotten to dream. Or perhaps you have let go of your dreams because it seems like it is taking too long for them to come true. Try that vision board, maybe you are scared to dream big, ok well then small dreams first, easily obtainable.

You can work your way up from here. Go ahead, dream, let loose, desire something more than your everyday grind, you deserve it.

25

MAKE A WISH

If wishes were dishes boy, I would be that fine, fine china.

Dandelion fluff, wishbones, stars, birthday candles and 11:11. You name it we wish on it. Do you believe deep in your core that wishes we make come true? Wishes granted are everyday joys, hopes and dreams coming into fruition.

Give in to the manifesting of your wishes. As children we are eager to watch our wishes come true, fully giving into the possibility. When we put something out into the universe it often has a way of coming back to us. The universe only wants what is best for us, it might not be exactly what we wanted, or expected, but it is usually exactly what we need. So go ahead; make a wish on a shooting star, toss a penny in a fountain, and wish for whatever your heart desires with childlike wonder and belief.

REVERSE

You believe in hard work and earning what you desire.

That is ok, and most likely what you have been taught by society. But today we are taking a step out of the norm! We are challenging you to find a dandelion, wish on a star, and let your wish go into the world, set it free! If you bottle them all up, how do you expect them to be heard or seen, how do you expect them to come to fruition? You cannot make all these wishes you bottled up come about alone! Let the universe aid you!

Even if you are not expecting results, how wonderful it will be when it does come true.

26

BOUND FOR BOUNDARIES

Cross this line, I dare you… It is time to put up your fences, set boundaries and keep them in place.

Now is the time to know what your boundaries are. Sometimes we do things to please people or avoid conflict, it's acceptable to close your gates and say no or no more. Everyday situations sometimes have us stretching our boundaries, whether at work or home. This can leave you feeling uncomfortable, it can leave you feeling somewhat resentful, or perhaps even leave you feeling like everybody's doormat.

You have permission as the captain of this ship to recognise this moment and steer clear of it.

REVERSE

Sometimes we set our boundaries so firmly that we do not give an inch.

There could be something rewarding outside your gate, so today make it a line in the sand and know when it is ok to just set that boundary a little less permanent. Sometimes the things knocking at the door are opportunities from the universe for us to grow and experience new things, if we are always hiding behind our fences from fear of past experience, we will never know what new and exciting things are seeking us out.

Just remember to have faith in yourself and know that it is always ok to say no and remove yourself from an uncomfortable or inappropriate situation.

27

GIVE IT A WHIRL

NEW AND IMPROVED! Try something new, who knows… you might like it! Settling into a comfort zone makes your horizon awfully dull and monotonous. Let's try a new hobby or even just walking down a different street on your way home! Being spontaneous can recharge the soul, give you a newfound passion for something, think of all the possibilities! All you have to do is try, because if you do not you will never know what could have been. You might just be unlocking something you didn't even know you were missing out on.

REVERSE

Are you dizzy from all the 'circles' you've been running in?

Never sticking with something, and constantly trying new things, well kudos but also NO. This isn't one of those 'throw everything you got at the wall and see what sticks' moments. Sometimes it takes a moment or a week to get the hang of something. If you finally master something (or at least figure it out) you will feel so rewarded. So, stick with it just a little longer.

28

FACE THE MUSIC

Hello music, I came to dance!

Well, you've done it and now you must face the music.

There are always ramifications to certain actions. It is SO important to learn to take responsibility for what you do. Take time to tackle the hard to look at fragments of your life, as well as owning your behaviour, and choices.

Buck up baby and remember, sometimes facing the music is easier than you might think.

In fact, it might be just the song you need! Sitting with an uncomfortable tune can help us grow and evolve.

REVERSE

Are you apologising again?

Perhaps you are even apologising for other people's actions… what the fudge sauce, Mary? You really need to stop that.

First of all, you are hardly responsible for other people's actions or their behaviour.

Secondly, when you constantly apologise, the words 'I am sorry' can become like a skipping record. It loses meaning and is just annoying.

So, change your tune and realise when it's time to face the music.

29

HEAD OVER HEELS

LOVE, AMORE, JE T'AIME, this thing that makes our heart speed up, our pulse quicken, gives us endless butterflies in our stomach.

If you are in love, remember these moments, when you were head over heels, do not take your partner for granted when what you have now may have become comfortable. Shake things up, do something exciting, find the passion between you, and fall head over heels once more.

If you have just fallen in love, fuel that excitement, keep that head over heels feeling, keep that 'new' relationship always new and exciting!

Never go to bed angry, and relish in the fact that someone loves you for exactly who you are.

REVERSE

Taking love for granted can for sure be a way to live an unfulfilled life with someone you once were head over heels for.

Can you rekindle that flame and gain that flexibility that made you head over heels? Or has your relationship come to a stalemate, so rigid that neither one of you are willing to bend at all?

It might be time to look into counselling and sit down to figure out just how to reignite that fire.

30

AGAINST THE CLOCK

Time flies when you are having fun!

Well, ain't this the truth.

Time is a strange thing, some people say life is short, but it is the longest thing we'll ever do. Are you procrastinating, perhaps you have a deadline that needs to be met and you have waited until you are fighting with time to get things completed? Time is precious, so use it wisely.

Do what needs to be done so you can enjoy the moments in between to the fullest without stressing your time crunch.

REVERSE

Are you trying to cram so much into your days that you are not fully enjoying anything?

Again, do what MUST get done, then take time to lavish yourself, perhaps be lazy, read a book, do something creative, or commune with nature.

Enjoy the time you get as well doing what must be done. Remember 'life is not measured by the number of breaths we take, but by the moments that take our breath away'.

So, take advantage of the free time by having some fun!

31

CRY FOR THE MOON

Have you heard the moon can make you do crazy things?

True fact. Have you ever wanted something so bad that you would plead, or barter your soul? A need so strong that you would almost give up who you are? What have you allowed to have that much power over you?

Sometimes, when something we want is out of reach or impossible, it is for a good reason. It's not that we don't deserve it, or that we aren't worthy of the things we want. It is often that the universe has to make room for something even better in our lives. Something that maybe we don't even realise we need.

REVERSE

We sometimes get lost in mania, desire, want, or need.

It can make us figuratively 'lunatics'. Know your worth and do not sell yourself short for something you desire. Once you truly understand your worth, you may realise that what you thought you wanted then, has nothing to do with you, it may not even align with your confident self. The moon is a powerful energy, and its back is shrouded in shadows and secrets, so before you get looney get CONFIDENT!

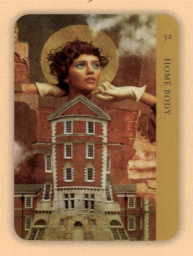

32

HOME BODY

Home – it is where the beings we love are, our cosiest pyjamas reside, filled with safety and love.

So today we give you permission to stay in and do the little things that you love: read a book, do some gardening, lavish in a bath, or perhaps do nothing at all. Today put the body in Home Body.

REVERSE

Now don't get us wrong, there is nothing like home, but there is a big wide world out there, new faces to see, new delights you have yet to try.

Shed your Home Body today, go on an adventure, make some new memories. Remember you might leave home, but home is where the heart is.

33

DUCKS IN A ROW

You quack me up. No seriously.

Look at your duckies, just making a mess everywhere.

Take time to get your life in order by getting organised and putting all of your ducks in a row. They can make it a point to avoid chaos, clutter and mishaps, as this will help you feel clarity. So, prioritise, declutter, get it together! Funny enough, when you are organised, it leaves room for more ducks.

So much chaos and unorganised life could lead to frenzy and anxiety. Leaving you overwhelmed and feeling helpless. We assure you that once you start lining up your duckies, everything will begin to fall into place much easier.

Maybe start with the smaller responsibilities and obligations then work your way up.

REVERSE

We interrupt this madness to bring you shelves!

Oh, look at you, bravo, so organised. Your ducks are lined up so lovely.

But are you so organised that you have lost all those wonderful spontaneous moments? Maybe the thought of doing something unscheduled intimidates you?

We give you permission to go out and do something unscheduled and fun.

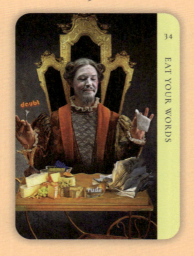

34

EAT YOUR WORDS

HANGRY?

Well, you better taste those words before you consume them.

Sometimes all sorts of things come out of people's mouths, maybe you think being snarky or rude is cute or funny? But here is the real. You never know what someone is going through. EVERYONE is going through something (that is relative to them) and we never know quite how they will digest your words.

A kind word can go a long way in the era of 'Karen and Ken', so douse those words in sugar if you intend on eating them. Bitter words can make you cocky and gag.

REVERSE

We like big butts and we cannot lie.

Or maybe we don't when we are the butt of a joke, or if we are on the receiving end of someone's forked tongue.

We must learn that sometimes people have nothing nice to say, or don't believe in you. But you can take this as an opportunity, use this as fuel, make them eat their words! Prove them wrong about who they think you are, be the bigger person. Serve that sh!t right back to them on a silver platter with a side of salt!

35

NO STRINGS ATTACHED

Look at you giving freely of yourself, no strings attached. What a wonderful thing giving without the expectation of receiving in return.

When you are able to do this it is truly an authentic act, and when we live in authenticity, we create room for others around us to do so too. You truly give from the heart with no expectations of return. This has become such a rarity these days.

What a beautiful human you are!

REVERSE

All those strings and ulterior motives can tangle you up.

We create a web of situations, of people feeling obligated, resentful, or just uninterested in dealing with you.

Try to recognise when you are keeping score in certain situations, just cut all those strings tying you down from being a score counter and stop waiting for a return on your proverbial investment. Just let your expectations go freely into the ether.

What a great feeling it is.

36

TOO MANY HATS

TOO MANY HATS

I love me a good hat and look at you, wow you sure look good in a hat, or 12.

    You know though this doesn't mean you have to wear all the hats all the time. We know that so much is expected of us, sometimes to be all things to all people. We are given so much responsibility in so many aspects of our lives, that we are suffering from horrendous hat hair. Oh, and also it will lead you to spreading yourself too thin and being burnt out.

We are asking you today, to recognise that you are bogged down with too many hats and hang some (or even one) on the hat rack.

Run your fingers through your hair and feel that weight lifted.

REVERSE

Everybody needs a hat or two. Look at you completely hatless!

Shirking your obligations, but for how long?

Let's go try on a visor, it will block the shine of that which distracts you. It is easy to get caught up in diversions which are shiny and easy. But you have some responsibilities to tend to.

Today try to stay focused and on track; do not get sidelined.

37

COUNT YOUR CHICKENS
BEFORE THEY HATCH

Ohhh my, look at this egg-cellent, oblong goody! 'Eggs!'

Are you the fox in your own hen house? Stealing those eggs and hiding them so you count on nothing?

We have to keep in mind that not all of these 'eggs' will come into fruition; so let's not count on all of them to hatch. In this age it is easy to crack that 'egg' to online order or pay someone for a service without actually keeping track of what you have left. It is so easy to overextend your bank roll and need more. When you make promises or plans based on what could happen you are bound to disappoint or end up in an uncomfortable and needy situation.

Sometimes it is best to wait, see what happens, and then act based on the result. If you are always 'writing cheques that can't be cashed', how can you survive?

Take time to just tend to the eggs you have.

REVERSE

Ohhh my, look at all your little chickadees, you have waited for ALL the eggs to hatch and now are just a hoarder of chickens… (there is a filthy joke in there somewhere). Stop blocking yourself from enjoying some of the finer things, or maybe just replace some of the broken things around you. It is fine to save for a rainy day, but when you live in the desert there is bound to be little to no rain.

This is giving you permission to splurge, even if it is a teensie, weensie purchase.

38

FOREVER YOUNG

Ahh the good old days when they would go door to door and peddle youth in the form of makeup.

Oh, of course you don't remember that you are so youthful. What we do to stay ever youthful and perky. There are gels, creams, surgeries, pills, fat freezing, etc, etc.

Take a day off from the two-hour beauty routine and put that retinol serum away (just for the day)!

It's your spirit, the joy and light that flows effortlessly through you that keeps you forever young. For instance, when you have been happy and then people tell you that you are radiant and glowing. You'll never have any time to share your glow with others if you're stuck behind a facial mask and a two-hour beauty routine! I mean there is a reason why where we do grooming is called a 'vanity'.

REVERSE

It's ok to take up a seat at the kids table, to fool around and be silly, but don't get stuck there.

Sometimes we chase youth because we are afraid of failing as an adult, afraid of responsibility, or of disappointing the people around us; and sometimes we are chasing youth because it was taken from us. It is truly easy to forget your age in these cases.

Today do one adult thing! Pay a bill early, send out that thank you card that's been shoved to the side.

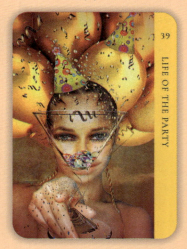

LIFE OF THE PARTY

HOORAY! Here you are, fashionably late and all. Everything about you is bright, full of light and laughter! Shine baby shine and spread that sparkle all over the place. You are the belle of the ball, the man of the hour, the life of the party!

Own your light, it is sometimes like a beacon in the dark to those who really need it. You are a true ray of sunshine that is much needed in this world.

Cheers luv, we are so glad you are here.

REVERSE

Oh, are you sweating? It can get hot under all those spotlights.

We sometimes mask our pain so that we can be the class clown or the life of the party. You have to take time to be true to yourself and how you are feeling in this moment. It's ok to take a step back, because when you do it allows others to 'hit their mark' and find their spotlights.

Give up the adulation for someone else while you take a much-needed breather and recharge your light.

Don't worry about the party for now.

40

BLESSING IN DISGUISE

Awww no… did you just lose that toxic person your loved ones have been warning you about?

Guess what that is AMAZING NEWS! Or perhaps that dead end job has sent you packing? HOORAY, celebrate!

Sometimes we cannot see an opportunity for what it truly is.

Have you recently lost a job, been turned down for a gig, or bombed on a date? Then think of it as the universe removing something from your path so that it can send you what you truly deserve! Sometimes we become comfortable or feel unworthy, so we stay put, afraid to look for those blessings.

Now is the time to think about what change you could benefit from that might feel a wee bit uncomfortable. We absolutely know it can be terrifying to walk away from a long-time comfort zone, even if we were miserable there.

We ask you to be fearless. Be the hero of your own story.

REVERSE

HUMAN… pity party of one…

Are you so stuck in misfortune or loss that you cannot see that this had to happen to make room for better things?

Change can be scary, or sometimes make you feel less worthy. But let's lighten the grip and just let go! What haunts you that you must live in this misfortune?

It is time to acknowledge what was lost and open your heart to the blessings of the universe. After all, we are just about sold out of your pity party decorations here.

41

PULL YOURSELF TOGETHER

Oh Mary… you are hot – a hot mess that is.

Your emotions are all over the place, and I'm not talking about your prolific use of emojis.

Take some time today to ground yourself in meditation or deep breathing. A whole is only as strong as its parts, and right now your emotional team has run amok!

Pieces of you left in the ether? Let us just pluck them up and start piecing yourself together. When you are not whole, how can you give yourself to something or someone? Do you feel pulled in many directions, and never enough to fulfill it all?

Take a moment, press pause and connect with yourself, and with your inner spirit. When you find your centre you will realise that you can pull yourself together. Do the work because it is time to get yourself together.

REVERSE

Aren't you the pillar of sh!t togetherness?

You just got it all figured out, huh? Stop tamping everything down, because hunny, you will lose it one day. I mean we are giving you full permission to let go, give in to your emotions. Even if it is to scream into your pillow, eat a tub of ice cream, or have a good cry.

We aren't really worried about you wallowing since it seems so hard to give in to emotion in the first place.

THIRD EYE BLIND

THIRD EYE BLIND

'I don't see with a third eye!'

Oh baby, open that eye, it really allows you to see through all the bullsh!t. Stop ignoring your instincts, your intuition, and insight!

Scared that it is just wishful thinking? Open that third eye and you will be surprised at all the foresight you have within you.

That gut feeling is your true north telling you to stop being blind. We have been so conditioned that there are only five senses but look at animals hearing things we cannot or seeing things we don't. We believe that the reason you are closed off is because it is all relative to your experiences, if you can't 'see' it tangibly then how could it be there?

Try some simple meditation to help you relax and get your 'inner eyesight' back.

REVERSE

You've got the gift (and there is no receipt for returns), but how do you share it?

You are open to the messages that spirit has to share, the whispered knowing in your ear. Now is the time to trust the messages. We often ask, 'but how do I know it's valid, and not just my imagination?' Trust and believe that messages from your 'Spiritual Team' won't be one off postcards.

If they need to say something they will find a way to get it to you, in a way that makes sense to you.

43

SPILL THE TEA

Mmmm, we love a good tea party, purr-whoops!

   Your tea has been spilt by another. Secrets and rumours have a way of flowing out like Georgia sweet tea. Hot or iced they grow stronger the longer they brew. Now is the time to get ahead of it, accept it and move on, even a tea party has an end. If you know your own truth, then it really doesn't matter what manure is spread on your proverbial lawn.

   Take this as a teaching moment to grow rather than simmer and rethink your circle of 'friends'.

REVERSE

Hey, is your name Gabby? Because you sure can be a complete gossip.

Living in the rumour mill and slinging dirt seems to bring you some twisted joy.

Take a step back and understand what you are doing could cause another person damage and realise that you might be lingering a little too long in the shade with a tipped teapot to make yourself feel better.

Take inventory on this and figure out how to make yourself happy. We usually tend to talk about others when we don't like exactly where we are at.

44

MANIFEST YOUR MIRACLE

Dandelions, wishbones, four-leaf clovers, OH MY!

Manifesting has always been a part of your life. Along the way we can find these practices childish, naive or taboo; but why?

What changed your perspective about manifesting your miracles?

This next bit is something we believe so strongly in. We as humans are energy, we are giving off a specific frequency, and that is the hum that is manifesting and bringing to life what we radiate.

So, set your intention and truly believe that it is yours and it is coming to you. You deserve to live the life you want.

Take this card as a sign that you are worthy. Step into your power and manifest your miracle.

(If you are a visual person then take time to create a vision board, the sky's the limit!)

REVERSE

'Miracles aren't a thing?' Pishaw.

Have you ever put something into the universe like a thought or a creative idea, then suddenly you are seeing this thought elsewhere, or this creative project on someone else's feed? Or perhaps you have bumped into that person you haven't seen in forever but were just thinking about?

Silently, in your mind, you set an intention and it travelled through the universe, boomeranging right back to you.

This is to let you know the universe is listening and ANYTHING is possible. Take your hint, go and manifest the heck out of your miracle.

ABOUT THE CREATORS

JENA DELLAGROTTAGLIA
ARTIST & CO-AUTHOR

Jena Dellagrottaglia has been creating oracle and tarot decks for several years and with some of the most well-known authors and publishers. Through digital mediums Jena has designed over a dozen decks and has been featured in *Oprah Daily* and many other design outlets. Her artwork has been featured on creative furniture pieces as well as greeting cards and more. This deck is her first as both an author and artist and she is excited to create more!

www.autumnsgoddess.com
Instagram @Jena_dellagrottaglia

LAURENCE TONER

CO-AUTHOR

Laurence grew up with a former English Professor as a parent, and it was through that he created a relationship with words. Laurence has been editing and crafting words for years creating print ads and materials, social media branding, and other literary projects both for professional and personal clients. As a young child Mr. Toner became fascinated with crystals and astrology. When he turned 11 he was gifted a beginners Tarot deck by a close friend.

'I am grateful to Jena for allowing me to work with her on this project. I sincerely believe that her art speaks for itself, but I am happy to put what I feel from that art into words to accompany it.' – Laurence

Instagram @WordsmithEdits

ACKNOWLEDGEMENTS

JENA

I would like to thank my soul sister Colette, for pushing me always to be better, and create my own work.

My husband for his never-ending support.

Thank you to Laurence, who saw my vision and believed in it so much that he hopped aboard for the ride!

Thank you to Lisa, for taking a chance on us, and helping bring our vision into fruition.

LAURENCE

I would like to thank Jena first and foremost for bringing this beautiful art into existence, and for believing in me enough to ask me to be a part of this collaboration. I am grateful to her, and to the amazing team at Rockpool who all do some amazing things to bring our work to life.